Words to Talk About

As you preview the stories for beginning readers, be sure to point out the following words and phrases not found in the story dictionaries.

W9-CCD-605

What Do You See?	I see
Turn Off the TV	please, turn off
Bath Time	takes
My Bed	put, room
Under an Umbrella	under
Here Comes the Net	swish
The Busy Pond	busy, jump, swim, quack, fly, play
Munch, Munch	lunch, crunch, school, hay
The Shortcut	catch, climb, let's, we'll
Are You Ready?	Are you ready?
Star Man	friend, stopped by, warm
The Ticket	teams, animals, game
Packing My Suitcase	spend the night, purple, clean
What Can You Put in It?	teacher, Ms. White
Shake Pudding	shake it up, quick, tight, thick
Trucks, Trucks, Trucks	do their jobs, haul, watch, work, hay, animals, corn, lights
The Campfire	sounds of the night, whispers, bright splash of light, awake, safe
The Polar Bear	paddles, North Pole, bottom, slipping, swimmer
Sam's Blue Hat	warm and soft, crowded, crawled
Animal Hide-and-Seek	Hide-and-Seek, meal, ocean, shell, match, different
Ally's Garden	pulled the weeds, raked, watered, soil, soft, planted, sprout, grow, worth it
Rainy Day Computer Fun	beeped, clicked, quiet, dark clouds, picture, moved, feel better
Zack's Sandwich	started

What Do You See?
Story Dictionary

can   man

kitten   truck

mitten   duck

My book:

EMC 638

I see a duck with a truck.

③

I see a kitten with a mitten.

✂

④

EMC 638

I see a man with a can.
That's what I see.

Name _____

What Did the Story Say?

Show what the girl saw.
Color. Cut. Paste.

duck ————

paste

paste

———— kitten

man ————

paste

What else could the girl see? Draw it on the back.

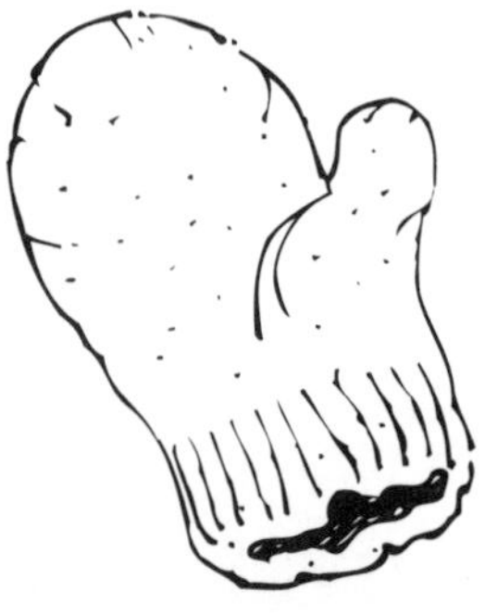

Name _____

Working with Word Families

-an

Write the word. Draw to show what each word means.

m + an = ___ ___ ___	c + an = ___ ___ ___
v + an = ___ ___ ___	f + an = ___ ___ ___
p + an = ___ ___ ___	t + an = ___ ___ ___

Read and Understand Grade 1 EMC 638

Name _____

Rhyming Pairs

Color, cut, and paste to show pairs that rhyme.

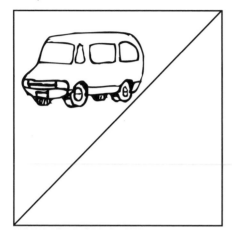
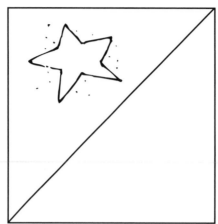

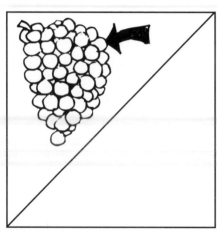
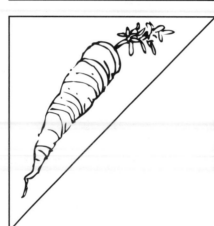
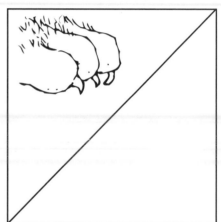

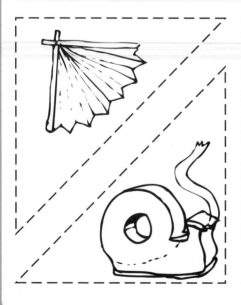

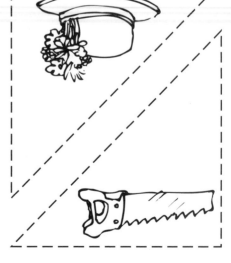

8

Name _____

Real or Make-Believe?

Could this be real? Circle Yes or No.

Yes   No

Yes   No

Yes   No

Yes   No

Yes   No

Yes   No

Turn Off the TV

Story Dictionary

Addy

 **Gramps**

Mom

My book:

EMC 638

Mom said, "Please turn off the TV."

©1997 by Evan-Moor Corp.

Gramps said, "Please turn off the TV."

Addy said, "Please turn off the TV."

EMC 638

What Did the Story Say?

Draw and write to show you remember what the story said.

1. What was Addy doing at the beginning of the story?

2. Show three things Addy could do when the TV is off.

3. Who was watching TV at the end of the story?

Rhyme Time

Put an **X** on the things that rhyme with **please**.

13

Name _____

On & Off

Write **On** or **Off** by each picture.

Name _____

More Than One Choice

Addy's mom and Gramps wanted her to turn off the TV. Draw four things that you could do at your house instead of watching TV.

If my mom said, "Please, turn off the TV," I could.....	If my mom said, "Please, turn off the TV," I could.....
If my mom said, "Please, turn off the TV," I could.....	If my mom said, "Please, turn off the TV," I could.....

Bath Time

Story Dictionary

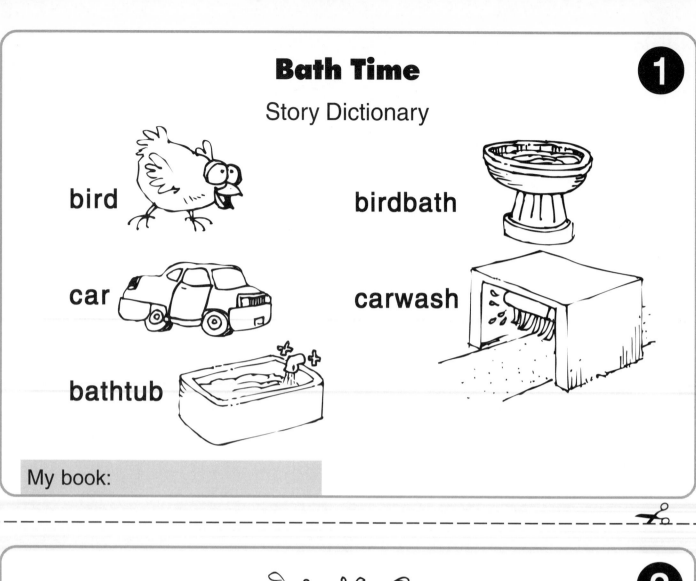

bird

birdbath

car

carwash

bathtub

My book:

EMC 638

The bird takes a bath in the birdbath.

The car takes a bath in the carwash.

I take a bath in the bathtub.
Mommy gets a bath too.

What Did the Story Say?

Draw to show what happened to Mommy.

Working with Word Families

-ar

c + ar = ___ ___ ___

Draw a car.

j + ar = ___ ___ ___

Draw a jar.

st + ar = ___ ___ ___

Draw a star.

b + ar = ___ ___ ___

Draw a boy on the bar.

Name _____

Different Places to Take a Bath

Cut and paste to show where each thing might take a bath.

- ✂

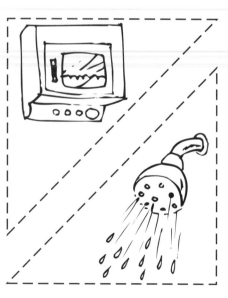

20

Name _____

A Funny Bath

Draw a funny bath.

Write or tell about the funny bath.

_____

_____

_____

_____

My Bed

Story Dictionary

blanket

books

bunny

My book:

I put my bunny in bed.

I put my blanket in bed.

EMC 638

I put my books in bed.
Is there room for me?

Name _____

What Did the Story Say?

In the story the boy put three things in his bed. Draw them here.

What else needed to be in bed? Draw it here.

Show three things you might put in your bed.

Read and Understand Grade 1 EMC 638

Name _____

Working with Word Families
-un

b + un = ____ ____ ____   f + un = ____ ____ ____

s + un = ____ ____ ____   g + un = ____ ____ ____

r + un = ____ ____ ____   p + un = ____ ____ ____

Use the words you made to complete these sentences.

Put the hot dog on the _____.

Playing is _____.

The _____ is hot.

Don't play with a _____.

The dogs _____.

Name _____

The Sound of P

Color the pictures that begin with the sound that **P** stands for.

Read and Understand Grade 1 EMC 638

A Fun Place to Sleep

Connect the dots to draw a place where it's fun to sleep. Start with 1 and count to 25.

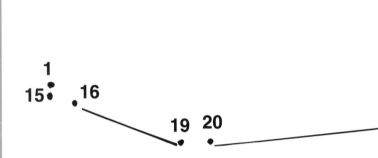
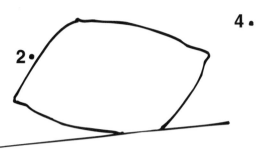
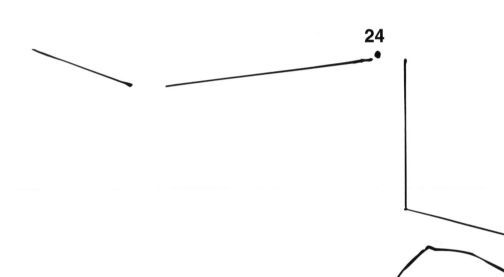
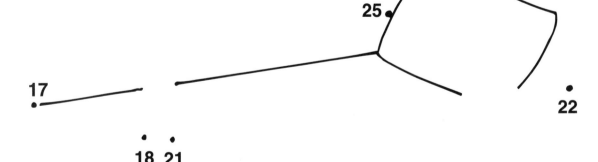
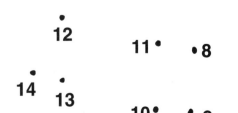

3 •

4 •

2 •

1
15 •   • 16

19   20

23 •

24 •

25 •

22 •

17 •

18 21

7 •

6   5

12 •

11 •   • 8

14   13

10 •   • 9

Under an Umbrella

Story Dictionary

bunny

man

dog

umbrella

My book:

EMC 638

The man is under an umbrella.

28

The dog is under an umbrella.

EMC 638

The bunny is under an umbrella too.

Name _____

What Did the Story Say?

Put the **X** on the word that is wrong.
Then draw a picture that goes with the story.

a woman under an umbrella

a dog under a blanket

the bunny is beside the umbrella

                                       Read and Understand Grade 1 EMC 638

Name _____

Working with Word Families

-og

d + og = ___ ___ ___  Do you have a dog? yes no	fr + og = ___ ___ ___  Are you bigger than a frog? yes no
l + og = ___ ___ ___  Can you jump the log? yes no	f + og = ___ ___ ___  Can you see in the fog? yes no
j + og = ___ ___ ___  Do you like to jog? yes no	h + og = ___ ___ ___  Do you eat like a hog? yes no

Name _____

Words That Tell Where

Circle the words to show where the bunny is.

under the box   on the box

under the log   on the log

under the wagon   on the wagon

under the pot   on the pot

under the bed   on the bed

under the chair   on the chair

32   Read and Understand Grade 1 EMC 638

Name _____

Following Directions

Read the color words. Color the umbrella.
Draw something under it.

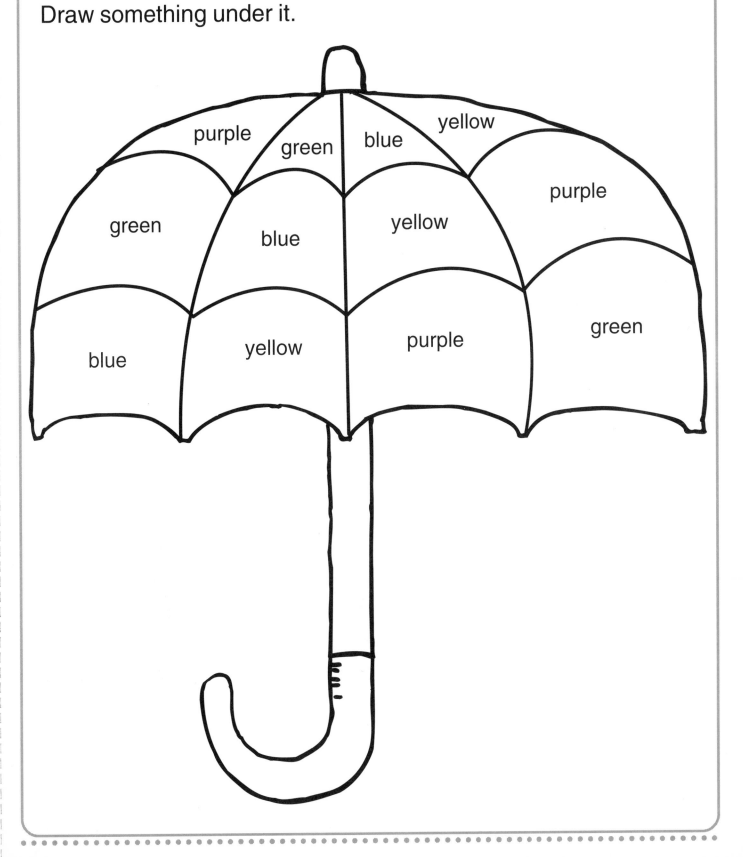

purple

green   blue   yellow

green   blue   yellow   purple

green

blue   yellow   purple

green

Read and Understand Grade 1 EMC 638

Here Comes the Net

①

Story Dictionary

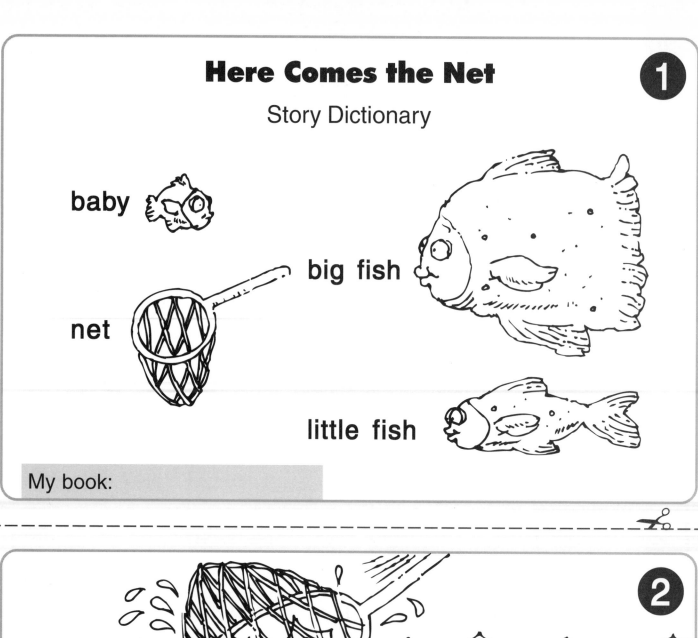

baby

net

big fish

little fish

✂

Swish, swish, big fish.
Here comes the big net.

②

EMC 638

Swish, swish, little fish.
Here comes the little net.

EMC 638

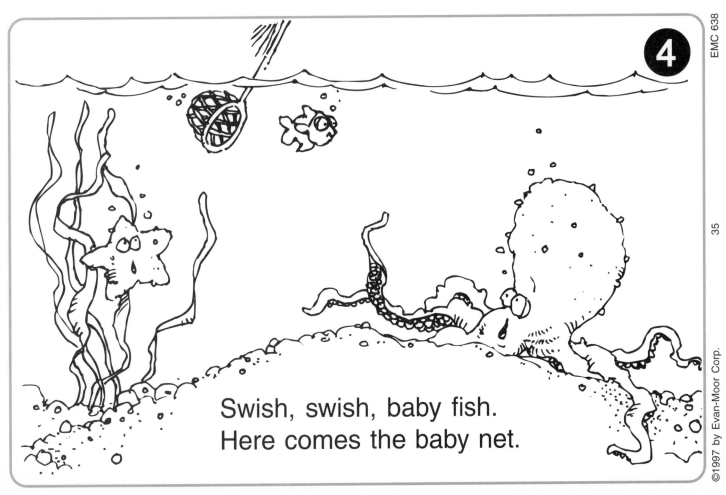

Swish, swish, baby fish.
Here comes the baby net.

Name _____

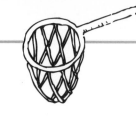

What Did the Story Say?

Draw to show what you think happened...

to the big fish.

to the little fish.

to the baby fish.

Name _____

Listening for Sounds

Color the pictures that begin with the sound that **sw** stands for.

Read and Understand Grade 1 EMC 638

Name _____

Swim or Fly

Look at the animals. Put them in two groups to show if they fly or if they swim.

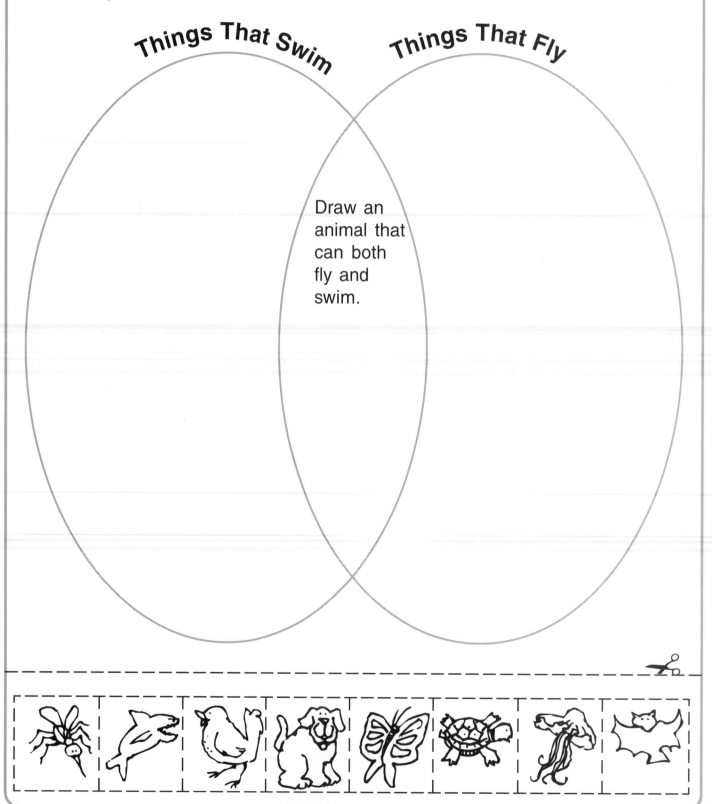

Things That Swim

Things That Fly

Draw an animal that can both fly and swim.

Read and Understand Grade 1 EMC 638

Name _____

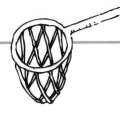

Working with Word Families
-ish

f + ish = ___ ___ ___ ___ ___ Draw a fish.	d + ish = ___ ___ ___ ___ ___  Fill the dish.
w + ish = ___ ___ ___ ___ Show your wish.	squ + ish = ___ ___ ___ ___ ___ ___ What goes squish?

The Busy Pond

1

Story Dictionary

bugs

fish

children

frogs

ducks

My book:

2

Busy pond.
The frogs jump.
The fish swim.

40

©1997 by Evan-Moor Corp.

Busy pond.
The ducks quack.
The bugs fly.

Busy pond.
The children play.

EMC 638

Name _____

What Did the Story Say?

Mark the things that made the pond busy.

Draw something new that might happen at the pond.

42

Name _____

Rhyme Time

Color, cut, and paste to show rhyming pairs.

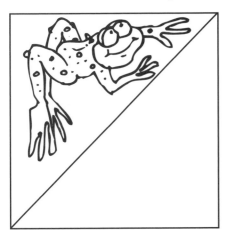  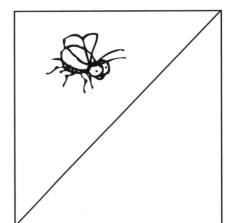

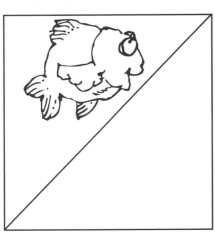 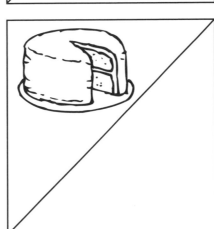 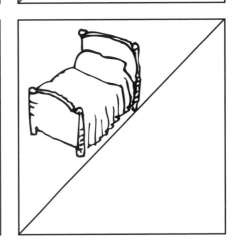

✂

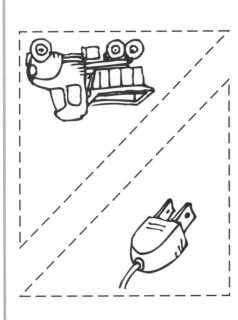 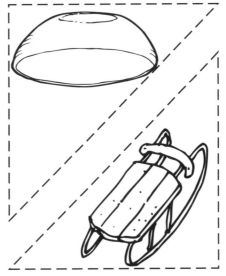 

43   Read and Understand Grade 1 EMC 638

Name _____

Real or Make-Believe?

Mark **yes** or **no**.

A duck can quack.	A duck can fly.	A duck can read.

yes no	yes no	yes no
A frog can color.	A frog can jump.	A frog can swim.
	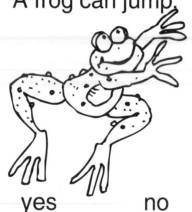	
yes no	yes no	yes no
A bug can hop.	A bug can paint.	A bug can run.

yes no	yes no	yes no

44

Name _____

The Sound of *d*

Color the pictures that begin with the sound that **d** stands for.
How many did you find? _____

Read and Understand Grade 1 EMC 638

Munch, Munch

Story Dictionary

1

children

goats

squirrels

My book:

2

See the goats?
They like to eat.
   Munch, Munch,
   Hay for lunch.

See the squirrels?
They like to eat.
Munch, Munch,
Hear the crunch.

EMC 638

See the children?
They like to eat.
Munch, Munch,
Good school lunch.

Name _____

What Did the Story Say?

Draw a line to show what the animals ate in the story.

squirrels   hay

goats   school lunch

children   nuts

Draw a picture to go with these words:

See the monkeys.   Munch, Munch,
They like to eat.   What a bunch!

Working with Word Families

-ay

Color, cut, and paste to show what each word means.

h + ay =	r + ay =	tr + ay =
_____	_____	_____
paste	paste	paste
cl + ay =	spr + ay =	pl + ay =
_____	_____	_____
paste	paste	paste

Write some other **-ay** words here.

_____

_____

✂ -

         Read and Understand Grade 1 EMC 638

Name _____

Munch, Munch

Some foods are noisy. Color the things that make crunchy noises when you eat them. Write MUNCH, MUNCH under the noisiest ones.

Name _____

My Favorite Lunch

Draw your favorite lunch.

Munch, Munch,

I eat _____ for lunch.

Read and Understand Grade 1 EMC 638

The Shortcut

Story Dictionary

butterfly

hilltop

woodpile

My book:

Let's take a shortcut.
We'll go to the hilltop.

EMC 638

52

©1997 by Evan-Moor Corp.

Let's take a shortcut.
We can catch a butterfly.

EMC 638

Let's take a shortcut.
We can climb the woodpile.
Then we'll go home.

What Did the Story Say?

Write and draw your answers to these questions.

Where did the shortcut go?

What did the boys catch?

What did they climb?

What do you think will happen next?

Working with Word Families
-ake

c + ake = ___ ___ ___ ___   sn + ake = ___ ___ ___ ___ ___

r + ake = ___ ___ ___ ___   sh + ake = ___ ___ ___ ___ ___

br + ake = ___ ___ ___ ___ ___

st + ake = ___ ___ ___ ___ ___

Use the new words to finish these sentences:

I used a _____ to pile up the leaves.

Pull on the _____ to stop the sled.

Molly will have a birthday _____.

The little _____ was green.

Mix milk and ice cream to make a _____.

The Sound of sh

Color the pictures whose names begin with the sound that **sh** stands for.

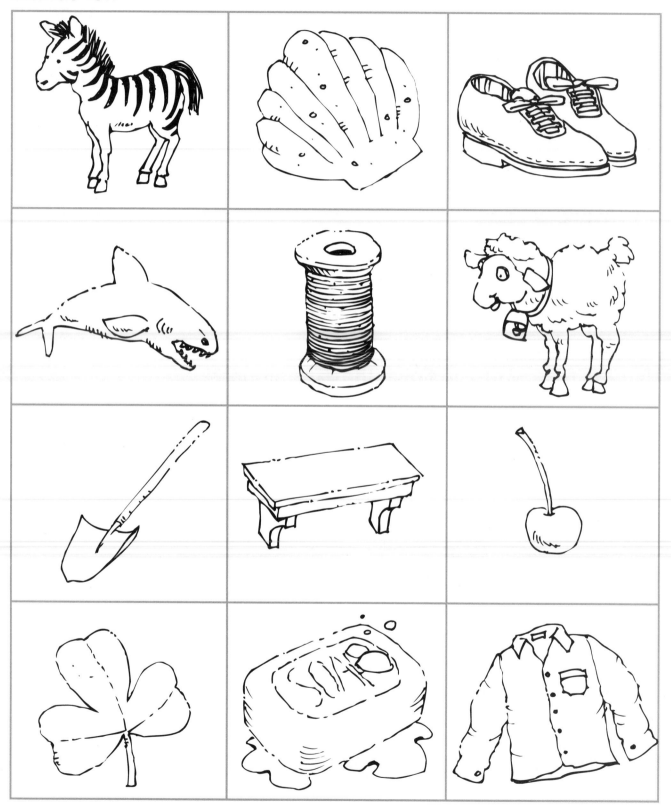

56

Name _____

Compound Words

Each of these words is made from two other words. Write the two words that make each compound word.

butterfly		_____ + _____
cupcake		_____ + _____
hilltop		_____ + _____
woodpile		_____ + _____
bathtub		_____ + _____
birdbath		_____ + _____
carwash		_____ + _____

Read and Understand Grade 1 EMC 638

Are You Ready?

Story Dictionary

black

checked

spotted

striped

white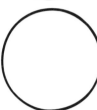

My book:

Black coat?   No.
White coat?   No.
Striped coat?   Yes!

Are you ready?   No.

EMC 638

White boots?	No.
Black boots?	No.
Spotted boots?	Yes!
Are you ready?	No.

4

EMC 638

Black hat?	No.
White hat?	No.
Checked hat?	Yes!

Are you ready?   Yes! I'm ready to go.

What Did the Story Say?

Color the clothes to show what the girl picked.
Circle the words that tell about the clothes.

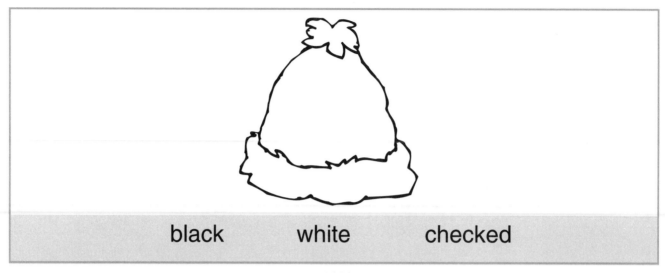

black   white   checked

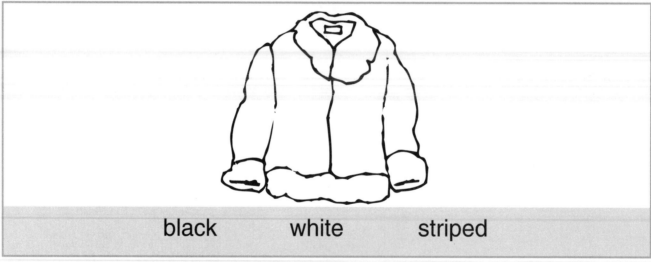

black   white   striped

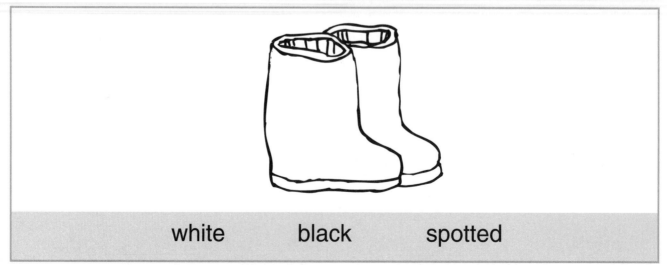

white   black   spotted

Working with Word Families
-at

c + at = ____ ____ ____   b + at = ____ ____ ____

Draw a cat with a bat.

h + at = ____ ____ ____   r + at = ____ ____ ____

Draw a rat with a hat.

f + at = ____ ____ ____   fl + at = ____ ____ ____ ____

Draw something that is fat.   Draw something that is flat.

Think and Draw

Show what might happen if your dad asked, "Are you ready?"

Show what might happen if your teacher asked, "Are you ready?"

Name _____

Match the Pairs

Match the pairs of socks. Paste them in the right boxes.

white socks	striped socks

spotted socks	checked socks

Star Man

Story Dictionary

cookies

Star Man

milk

window

My book: _____

EMC 638

Hey, Star Man.
I see you from my window.
You are my friend.

I've been thinking...
Do you have a bed?
Does your mom bring you warm milk?
Do you eat cookies, too?

I see you from my window.
I'm glad that you stopped by.
Good night, Star Man.

EMC 638

Name _____

What Did the Story Say?

What questions did the boy ask Star Man?

_____

_____

_____

What questions would you ask?

_____

_____

_____

Working with Word Families
-ed

T + ed = ____ ____ ____

sl + ed = ____ ____ ____ ____

r + ed = ____ ____ ____

Draw Ted sitting on a red sled.

b + ed = ____ ____ ____

Fr + ed = ____ ____ ____ ____

Draw Fred sleeping in his bed.

N + ed = ____ ____ ____

sh + ed = ____ ____ ____ ____

Draw Ned painting his shed.

Rhyme Time

Circle the two pictures in each line that rhyme.

1

2

3

4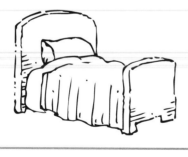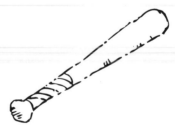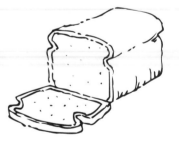

5

Read and Understand Grade 1 EMC 638

Name _____

Questions and Answers

Write a sentence to answer the questions.

Do you have a dog?

_____

Do you like pizza?

_____

Do you eat apples?

_____

Do you play ball?

_____

Write your own question. Have a friend answer it.

_____

_____

_____

_____

 Read and Understand Grade 1 EMC 638

The Ticket

Story Dictionary

football

ticket

movies

zoo

My book:

I have a ticket.
I will go to the football game.
I will see the teams play.

❸

I have a ticket.
I will go to the movies.
I will buy some popcorn.

✂ -

❹

EMC 638

I will go to the zoo.
I will see the animals.
I have two tickets.
Will you come too?

Name _____

What Did the Story Say?

Where did the first boy go?

_____

_____

Where did the girl go?

_____

_____

Where did the last boy go?

_____

_____

Would you go to the zoo too?

_____

_____

Draw to show a place where you would need a ticket.

Where Would You Find It?

Cut and paste to show where you would find each thing.

At a Football Game	
At the Movies	
At the Zoo	

Is there something that you would find at all these places? Draw it here.

Name _____

Color the Tickets

Read the color words on the tickets. Color to show you know what each word says.

 red

 orange

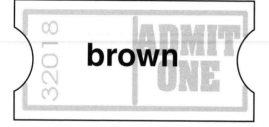 brown

 yellow

 black

 pink

 green

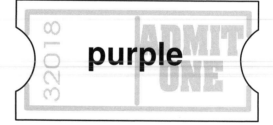 purple

 blue

Name _____

The Zoo

Color. Cut. Paste. Put the animals in their cages.

monkey   giraffe   elephant

tiger   hippo   bear

Packing My Suitcase

1

Story Dictionary

blanket

toothbrush

dinosaur pj's

teddy bear

pillow

socks

My book:

2

EMC 638

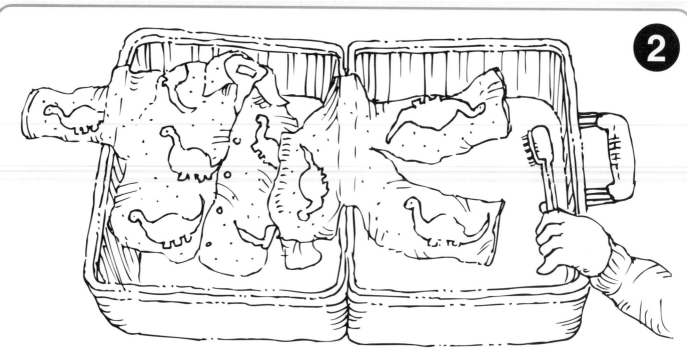

I'm going to spend the night at Grandma's.
I'll take my dinosaur pj's.
I'll take my purple toothbrush.

I'll take my blue blanket.
I'll take my teddy bear.
I'll take my clean socks.

EMC 638

I'll take my new book.
I'll take my soft pillow.
I'm going to spend the night at Grandma's.

What Did the Story Say?

Pack the suitcase to show what the story said.

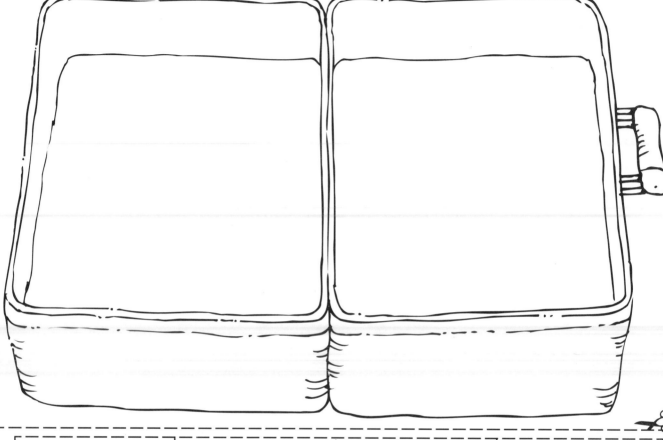

Read and Understand Grade 1 EMC 638

Working with Word Families
-ock

bl + ock = ___ ___ ___ ___ ___   cl + ock = ___ ___ ___ ___ ___

l + ock = ___ ___ ___ ___   r + ock = ___ ___ ___ ___

s + ock = ___ ___ ___ ___   d + ock = ___ ___ ___ ___

fl + ock = ___ ___ ___ ___ ___   kn + ock = ___ ___ ___ ___ ___

Write the words to label the pictures.

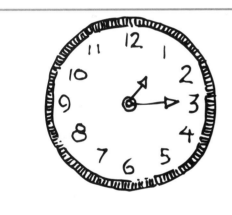

___ ___ ___ ___ ___

___ ___ ___ ___

___ ___ ___ ___ ___

___ ___ ___ ___

Name _____

Soft or Hard

Color, cut, and paste. Show which things are soft and which things are hard.

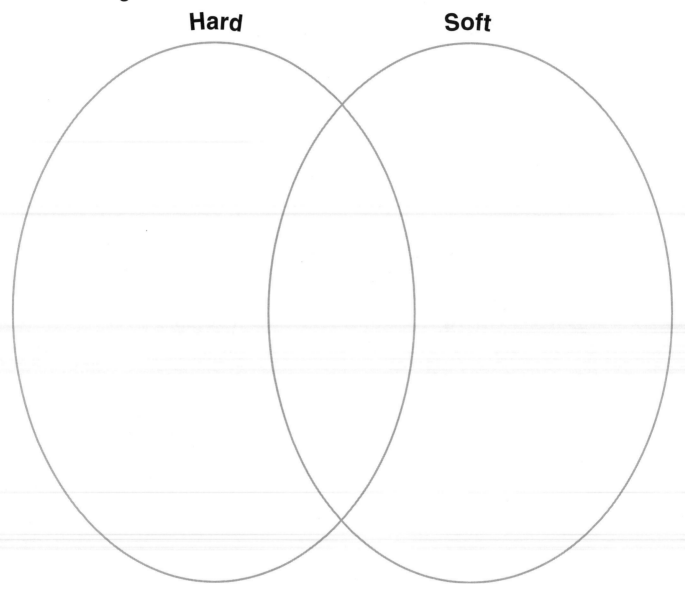

Hard   **Soft**

Is anything soft and hard at the same time? Put it in the middle section between soft and hard.

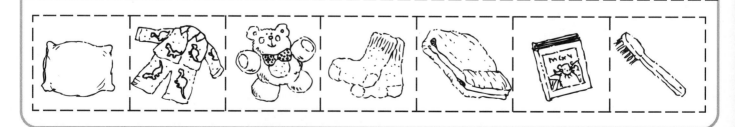

Read and Understand Grade 1 EMC 638

Name _____

My Suitcase

Pretend that you are going to spend the night at your Grandma's house. Show what you would pack.

Read and Understand Grade 1 EMC 638

What Can You Put in It?

Story Dictionary

bus

dragon

truck

wagon

rocks

quacking duck

shoe

My book:

What can you put in a wagon?
A box,
a bag,
and Willy's dragon.

EMC 638

82

©1997 by Evan-Moor Corp.

What can you put in a truck?

Some rocks,
a shoe,
and a quacking duck.

EMC 638

What can you put in a bus?
Ms. White,
Teacher,
and all of us.

What Did the Story Say?

Draw to show what went in each thing.

Name _____

Working with Word Families

-ag

b + ag = ____ ____ ____   fl + ag = ____ ____ ____ ____

t + ag = ____ ____ ____   dr + ag = ____ ____ ____ ____

r + ag = ____ ____ ____   z + ag = ____ ____ ____

Use your new **-ag** words to write compound words.

a bean_____	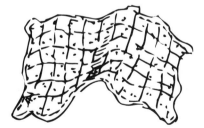
a _____pole	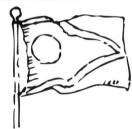
a dish_____	
a zig_____	

Name _____

What's at the End?

Write the letter that stands for the sound that you hear at the end of each word.

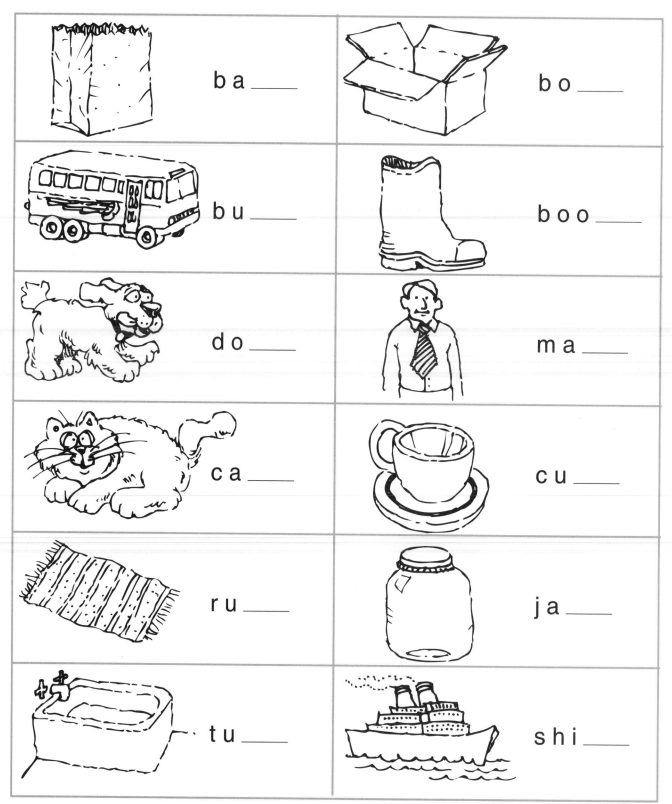

b a ___

b o ___

b u ___

b o o ___

d o ___

m a ___

c a ___

c u ___

r u ___

j a ___

t u ___

s h i ___

Read and Understand Grade 1 EMC 638

Make a Wagon

Color, cut, and paste to make a wagon.
Tell what you would haul in it.

Cut on solid lines.
Fold on dotted lines.

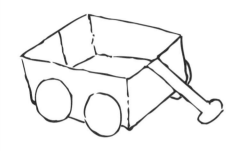

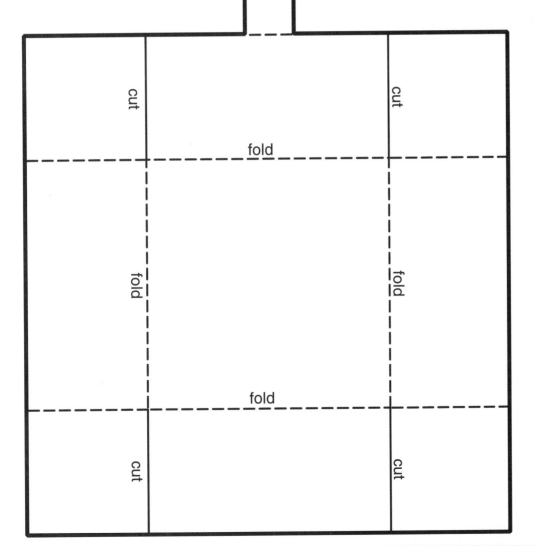

cut

cut

fold

fold

fold

fold

cut

cut

Read and Understand Grade 1 EMC 638

Shake Pudding

Story Dictionary

①

cup

spoon

lid

milk

My book:

✂

②

First put in the mix.
Add the milk just so.
Put on the lid and shake.

Shake it up.
Shake it up.
Shake it up fast.

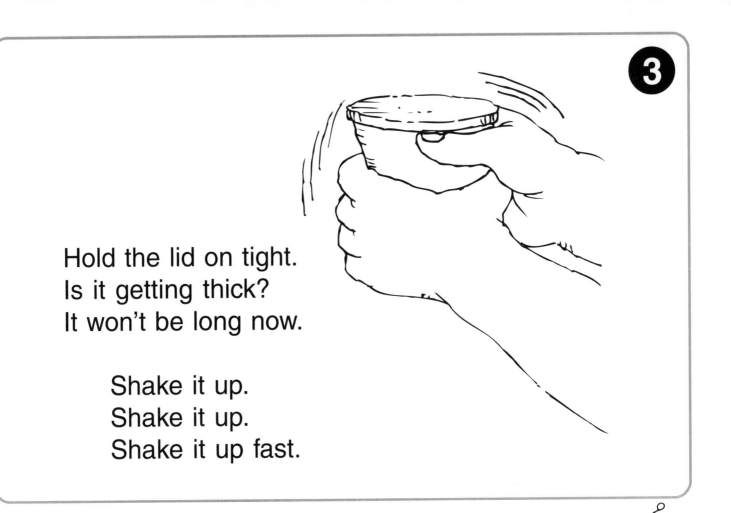

Hold the lid on tight.
Is it getting thick?
It won't be long now.

Shake it up.
Shake it up.
Shake it up fast.

EMC 638

Stop. Take off the lid.
Get a spoon and ...

Eat it up.
Eat it up.
Eat it up fast.

What Did the Story Say?

Put the steps in order.

1.

2.

3.

4.

5.

6.

✂

Eat it up.	Add the milk.
Shake it up.	Put in the mix.
Take off the lid.	Put on the lid.

Name _____

Will You Eat It?

Mom says, "Eat it up fast."
Draw to show what Mom
wants you to eat.

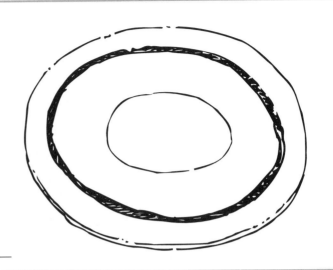

Will you eat it? _____

Will you eat it fast? _____

Dad says, "Eat it up fast."
Draw to show what Dad
wants you to eat.

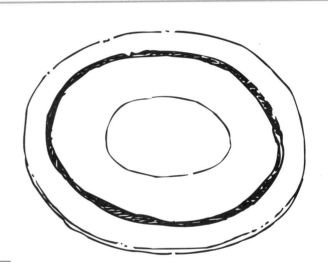

Will you eat it? _____

Will you eat it fast? _____

Brother says, "Eat it up fast."
Draw to show what Brother
wants you to eat.

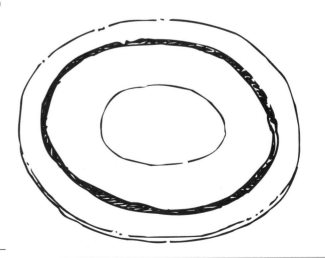

Will you eat it? _____

Will you eat it fast? _____

Rhyme Time

Cut out the circles. Punch holes.
String the pictures that rhyme on a
piece of string.

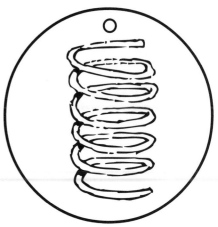

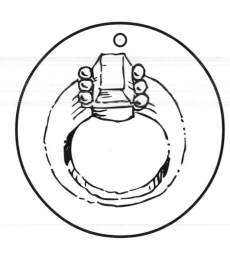

Name _____

Cooking Is Fun!

Connect the dots to see what the two cooks made.
Start with 1.

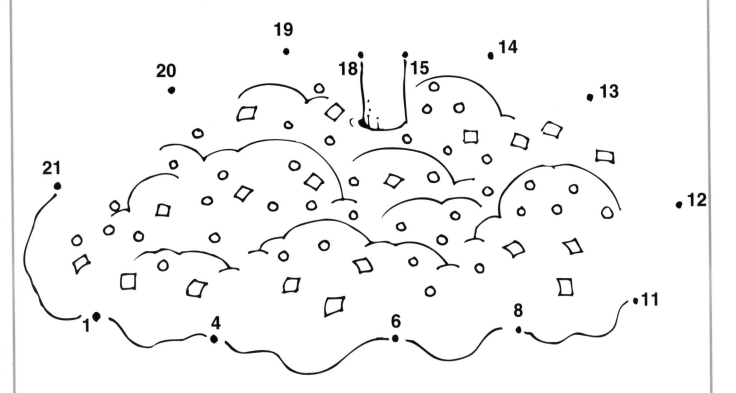

    Read and Understand Grade 1 EMC 638

Trucks, Trucks, Trucks

Story Dictionary

animals

blocks

lights

firemen

hose

ladders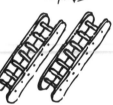

My book:

EMC 638

See the trucks, big and small.
Watch them work. They do it all.

Farm trucks help farmers to do their jobs.
    They haul hay.
    They haul animals.
    They haul corn.

Big rig trucks help people to do their jobs.
They haul gas.
They haul food.
They haul cars.

Fire trucks help firemen to do their jobs.
They haul ladders.
They haul hoses.
They haul lights.

EMC 638

Toy trucks help kids to do their jobs.
They haul blocks.
They haul dolls.
They haul friends.

See the trucks, big and small.
Watch them work. They haul it all.

What Did the Story Say?

Draw to show what the story said farm trucks haul.	Draw to show what the story said big rigs haul.
Draw to show what the story said toy trucks haul.	Think of one more thing that a toy truck could haul. Draw it here.

Opposites

Color, cut, and paste.
Sort the pictures to show which things are heavy and which things are light.

These things are heavy.	These things are light.
paste paste	paste paste
paste paste	paste paste

Adding -er

Add **-er** to these words. Draw a line from the new word to the picture that shows something for that person to use.

farm + er = __ __ __ __ __ __

build + er = __ __ __ __ __ __ __

paint + er = __ __ __ __ __ __ __

teach + er = __ __ __ __ __ __

jump + er = __ __ __ __ __

play + er = __ __ __ __ __ __

Write Another Page for Trucks, Trucks, Trucks

Write words in the blanks. Draw pictures.

_____ trucks help _____ do their jobs.

They haul _____.

They haul _____.

They haul _____.

The Campfire

Story Dictionary

campfire

sleeping bag

owl

My book:

The campfire is making a bright splash of light on the black night. The trees stand tall. I am in my sleeping bag. The sounds of the night keep me awake.

The wind whispers. The owl hoots. Something moves in the dark.

I hear the snap of the fire. I'm glad for its warm light. It makes me feel safe.

EMC 638

What Did the Story Say?

Where is the storyteller?

_____

_____

_____

_____

What is the storyteller doing?

_____

_____

_____

_____

Why does the storyteller like the campfire?

_____

_____

_____

_____

Camping

Look at the picture. Answer the questions.

Where's the boy? _____

_____

Where's the cook pot? _____

_____

Where's the sleeping bag? _____

_____

Where's the camp? _____

_____

Word Box	
in the forest	in the sleeping bag
in the tent	on the fire

Fire Words

Write the two words that work together in these compound words.

firefly   _____ + _____

campfire   _____ + _____

fireplace   _____ + _____

fireplug   _____ + _____

fireworks   _____ + _____

fireman   _____ + _____

fireboat   _____ + _____

firecracker   _____ + _____

bonfire   _____ + _____

firelight   _____ + _____

fireproof   _____ + _____

surefire   _____ + _____

fireside   _____ + _____

wildfire   _____ + _____

The Sound of spl

Draw something that would make a big splash.

Splish, splosh, splash!!

Draw something you can split.

Splot, splat, split.

Draw something that would splatter.

Splitter, splotter, splatter!

The Polar Bear

Story Dictionary

1

polar bear

warm fur coat

back legs

front legs

My book:

EMC 638

2

The polar bear lives near the North Pole. Every day it walks on the snow. It has fur on the bottom of its feet. The fur keeps its feet warm. The fur also keeps the bear from slipping on the snow.

Every day the polar bear swims in the cold water. The polar bear is a good swimmer. It paddles with its front legs. It pulls its back legs along.

EMC 638

After it swims, it shakes the water from its fur coat. BRRRR!

Name _____

What Did the Story Say?

Write four things that you learned about polar bears.

1. _____

2. _____

3. _____

4. _____

Think of another place a polar bear could live. Draw and tell about it.

Working with Word Families
-ear

b + ear = ___ ___ ___ ___   t + ear = ___ ___ ___ ___

w + ear = ___ ___ ___ ___   p + ear = ___ ___ ___ ___

Use the new words to complete these sentences.

The polar _____ likes cold places.

The shirt had a _____.

I will _____ my coat.

Did you eat the _____?

Write your own sentence using an **-ear** word.

_____

_____

_____

_____

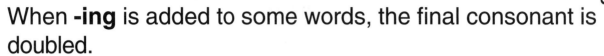

Name _____

Adding -ing

When **-ing** is added to some words, the final consonant is doubled.

slip + ing = slip(p)ing

Add **-ing** to these words.
Be sure to double the final consonant.

swim + ing = ___ ___ ___ ___ ___ ___ ___

run + ing = ___ ___ ___ ___ ___ ___

tap + ing = ___ ___ ___ ___ ___ ___

stop + ing = ___ ___ ___ ___ ___ ___ ___ ___

hit + ing = ___ ___ ___ ___ ___ ___ ___

flip + ing = ___ ___ ___ ___ ___ ___ ___ ___

Is there anything that is the same about each of these words?

_____

_____

_____

_____

A Polar Bear Crossword Puzzle

Across

1. The polar bear has white _____.

2. The _____ like to swim in the cold water.

4. Fur helps the bear stay _____.

Down

1. The polar bear has four _____.

3. The polar bear can _____ in cold water.

Word Bank		
swim	feet	warm
fur	bears	

       Read and Understand Grade 1 EMC 638

Sam's Blue Hat

Story Dictionary

bunny

fox

ladybug

mouse

goat

My book:

One day Sam lost his hat. It was a blue hat. It was soft and warm. It had a bell on its tip.

A little mouse saw the blue hat. It looked warm and soft. The mouse moved in.

A bunny saw the blue hat. It looked warm and soft. The bunny hopped in. The blue hat got bigger.

A fox saw the blue hat. It looked warm and soft. The fox went in. The blue hat got bigger.

A goat saw the blue hat. It looked warm and soft. The goat crowded in. The blue hat got bigger.

A ladybug saw the blue hat. It looked warm and soft. The ladybug crawled in.

EMC 638

Oh, no! The blue hat ripped.
The mouse was sad.
The bunny was sad.
The fox was sad.
The goat was sad.
The ladybug was sad.
All that was left was the little bell.

What Did the Story Say?

What happened to start the story?

_____

What happened to end the story?

_____

Folk tales like this one have been told over and over in many different ways. Change what is lost in the story and tell it again.

_____

_____

_____

_____

_____

_____

_____

Putting It in Order

Cut and paste to show the order that the animals moved into the hat.

First

paste

Fourth
paste

Second
paste

Fifth
paste

Third
paste

✂ -

When It Belongs to Someone

We use **'s** to show that something belongs to someone. The blue hat belonged to Sam so we say it was Sam's hat.

Circle the words with **'s**. Finish the sentence to tell what belongs to someone.

The bunny's ears were long.

The ears belong to the _____ .

The goat's horns were sharp.

The horns belong to the _____ .

The bunny stepped on the mouse's tail.

The tail belongs to the _____ .

The ladybug's wings folded across her back.

The wings belong to the _____ .

The ladybug's spots were black.

The spots belong to the _____ .

The fox looked in the bunny's home.

The home belongs to the _____ .

The goat and the mouse liked Sam's hat.

The hat belongs to _____ .

Big, Bigger, Biggest

Read all the boxes before you begin.

Draw a big balloon.	Draw a bigger balloon.
Draw the biggest balloon.	Show what happens to the biggest balloon.

Animal Hide-and-Seek

Story Dictionary

beaver

insect

chipmunk

mountain lion

deer

ray

turtle

My book:

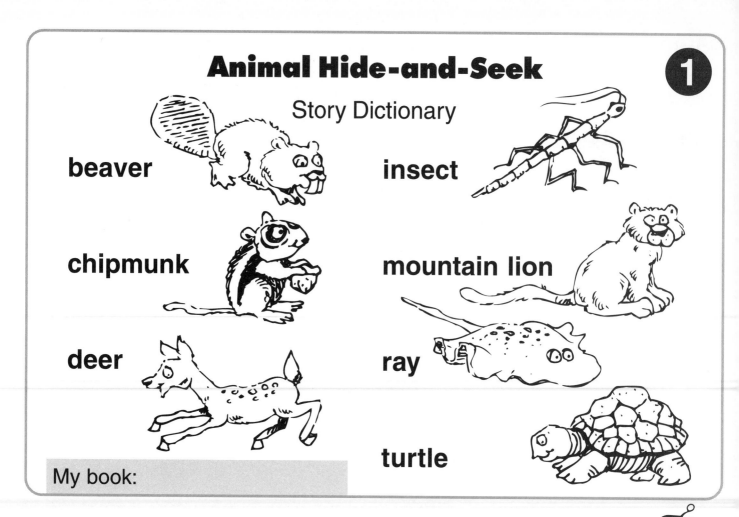

2

EMC 638

118

Have you ever played Hide-and-Seek?
For animals hiding is more than a game.
The mountain lion can hide behind a log.
It waits for a deer to pass.
The deer will be its next meal.

3

Hiding can keep animals safe too.
The chipmunk ducks into its hole.
The beaver swims into its home.
The ray hides in sand on the bottom of the ocean.
The turtle hides in a hard shell.

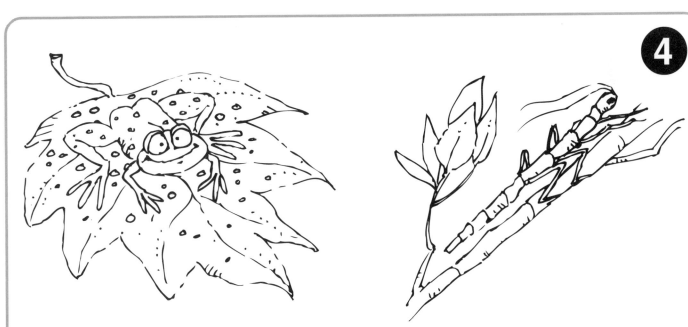

4

EMC 638

Other animals match the places they hide.
Think about the green frog on the green leaf.
Think about the insect that looks like a stick.
Hiding helps animals in different ways.

Name _____

What Did the Story Say?

List two reasons why animals hide.

_____

_____

Draw a line to show where each animal hides.

Animals	**Hiding Places**

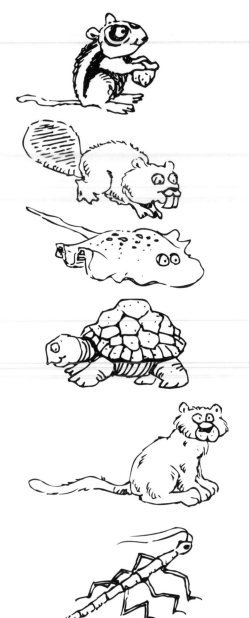

Read and Understand Grade 1 EMC 638

The Sound of i

Color the pictures that have the same vowel sound as hide.

The Game

Color and cut the pictures. On another paper, paste them in order to tell the story of the frog's game.

Camouflage

Some animals use color to help them hide. This is called camouflage. Try making your own camouflage animal.

- Color the two boxes below in the same way.
- Cut an animal out of the second box.
- Add an eye on the cutout.
- 123 Lay the animal cutout on the first box.
    Is your animal hard to see?
    Does the color help it hide?

Read and Understand Grade 1 EMC 638

Ally's Garden

Story Dictionary

beets

radishes

lettuce

water

My book:

Ally wanted a garden.
She pulled the weeds.
She raked the soil to make it soft.
Gardens are hard work.

3

Ally wanted a garden.
She planted the seeds.
She watered the seeds.
She saw little plants sprout and grow.
She gave them water.
Gardens are hard work.

4

EMC 638

Ally wanted to have a garden.
She picked lettuce.
She pulled radishes and beets.

Gardens may be hard work, but they're worth it.

What Did the Story Say?

What kind of seeds did Ally plant?

_____

What did Ally do to start her garden?

_____

_____

Is a garden fast or slow? Tell why you think the way you do.

_____

_____

Draw a garden that you might make. Show something you would do to take care of the growing plants.

Working with Word Families

-ant

Circle the word part that is the same.

plant

slant

pant

grant

chant

Put each word from the box in the puzzle.

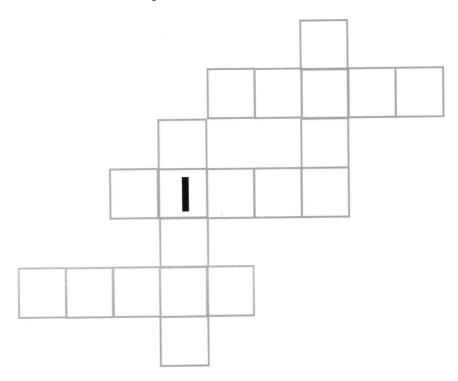

Put a word from the word box in each sentence.

It was hot so the dog began to _____.

I wonder what seeds I should _____.

The girls jumped rope as they shouted the _____.

The tower of blocks started to _____.

Name _____

Making a Garden

Put the steps in order. Write about the steps on another paper.

1	2
3	4

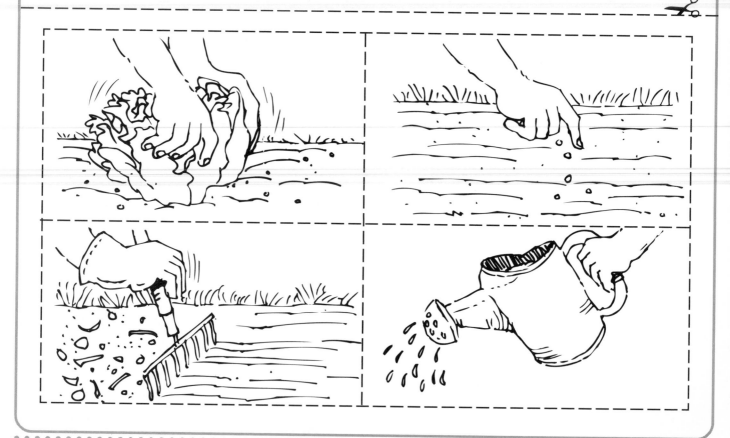

128   Read and Understand Grade 1 EMC 638

Name _____

Tools for Gardening

Match the tool to the job.

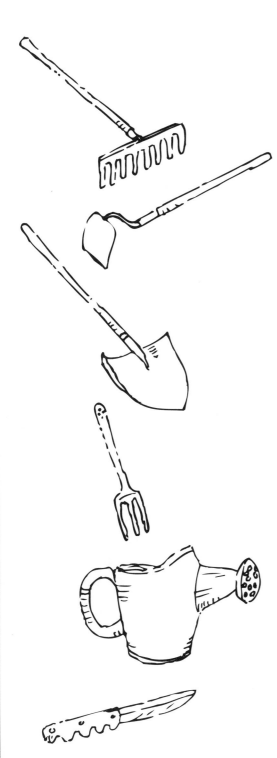

dig up the potatoes

make ditches for watering

cut off the greens

smooth the soil

water the seeds

eat the salad

Read and Understand Grade 1 EMC 638

Rainy Day Computer Fun

①

Story Dictionary

computer

mouse

window

mailbox

raining

My book:

---

②

EMC 638

It was quiet. Dark clouds covered the sun. Rain splashed on the window. Rhia was working at her computer. The computer beeped. A mailbox picture popped up. Rhia smiled. There was a letter in the computer mailbox. Rhia hoped that it was for her. She moved the mouse and clicked it. The e-mail came on the screen.

©1997 by Evan-Moor Corp.

Hi Rhia,
Is it raining at your house?
I have to stay inside because
I have a cold.
Send me an e-mail, please.

Your friend,
Tania

Rhia smiled again. The letter was for her. It was from her friend Tania. It must be raining at Tania's house too. And Tania had a cold. Rhia would write her a note now.

4

EMC 638

Dear Tania,
I got your e-mail.
It is raining at my house.
I'm sorry that you have a cold.
I hope the sun comes out.
Feel better soon.

Your friend,
Rhia

What Did the Story Say?

What kind of a day was it?

_____

What was Rhia doing?

_____

What is Tania doing?

_____

How did Rhia feel when she got the e-mail?

_____

What do you think will happen when Tania gets Rhia's e-mail?

_____

Who would you send an e-mail to?

_____

What would you say?

_____

_____

_____

Working with Word Families
-ail

h + ail = ___ ___ ___ ___   j + ail = ___ ___ ___ ___

m + ail = ___ ___ ___ ___   n + ail = ___ ___ ___ ___

qu + ail = ___ ___ ___ ___   sn + ail = ___ ___ ___ ___

t + ail = ___ ___ ___ ___   tr + ail = ___ ___ ___ ___

Draw a line from the picture to the word that names it.

hail

mail

quail

tail

jail

nail

snail

trail

133   Read and Understand Grade 1 EMC 638

Name _____

Put It in Order

Cut and paste to put the story events in order. Use another piece of paper. Write a sentence to tell what happens in each picture.

Rainy Day Fun

Make a list of things that you could do on a rainy day. Draw yourself doing one of the things on your list.

_____

_____

_____

_____

_____

Zack's Sandwich

Story Dictionary

ham

lettuce leaf

pickle

sandwich

slice of bread

My book:

This is Zack.

Here is a slice of bread
that started the sandwich
that Zack made.

This is the pickle
on top of a slice of bread
that started the sandwich
that Zack made.

This is the ham that
covers the pickle
on top of a slice of bread
that started the sandwich that Zack made.

This is the lettuce leaf
on the ham that
covers the pickle
on top of a slice of bread
that started the sandwich that Zack made.

EMC 638

This is another slice of
bread, a lid for the
lettuce leaf on the ham
that covers the pickle
on top of the slice of
bread that started the
sandwich that Zack
made.

This is the sandwich
that Zack made.

Name _____

What Did the Story Say?

Write a recipe for making Zack's sandwich.

Recipe for a Sandwich
From Zack's Kitchen

Ingredients:

_____ _____

_____ _____

What to do:

1. _____

2. _____

3. _____

4. _____

5. _____

Draw a picture to show how it will look when it is finished.

Working with Word Families
-ice

d + ice = ___ ___ ___ ___   m + ice = ___ ___ ___ ___

pr + ice = ___ ___ ___ ___ ___   sl + ice = ___ ___ ___ ___ ___

tw + ice = ___ ___ ___ ___ ___   n + ice = ___ ___ ___ ___

sp + ice = ___ ___ ___ ___ ___   r + ice = ___ ___ ___ ___

Write some sentences using the new **-ice** words.

_____

_____

_____

_____

_____

_____

Make a Hanging Sandwich

Color and cut the sandwich pieces.
Tie string to one slice of bread.
String ingredients.
Finish with second slice of bread.

Read and Understand Grade 1 EMC 638

Answer Key

Page 6
duck - truck
mitten - kitten
man - can

Page 8

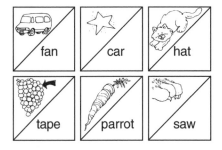

Page 9
Yes No
Yes No
No No

Page 12
1. Addy was watching television.
2. Answers will vary.
3. Answers will vary.
4. Gramps and Mom.

Page 13

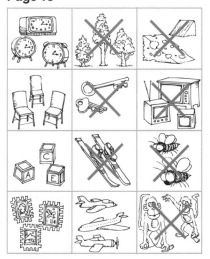

Page 14
On On
On Off
Off On
On Off

Page 20

Page 24
Pictures of bunny, blanket, books
Picture of the boy
Last section answers will vary

Page 25
bun fun
sun gun
run pun

Sentences:
bun
fun
sun
gun
run

Page 26

Page 27
picture shows a set of bunk beds

Page 30
a ~~woman~~ under an umbrella
picture should show a man under an umbrella

a dog under a ~~blanket~~
picture should show a dog under an umbrella

the bunny is ~~beside~~ the umbrella
picture should show bunny under umbrella

Page 32
under the box   on the log
under the wagon   under the pot
on the bed   on the chair

Page 37

Page 38

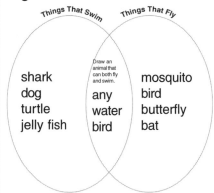

Page 42

Page 43

| dog | truck | plug |
| dish | rake | sled |

Page 44

A duck can quack.	yes
A duck can fly.	yes
A duck can read.	no
A frog can color.	no
A frog can jump.	yes
A frog can swim.	yes
A bug can hop.	yes
A bug can paint.	no
A bug can run.	yes

Page 45

Page 48

squirrels — hay
goats — school lunch
children — nuts

Page 50

MUNCH, MUNCH answers may vary.

Page 54

to the hilltop
a butterfly
the woodpile
answers will vary

Page 55

cake snake
rake shake
brake
stake

sentences:
rake
brake
cake
snake
shake

page 56

Page 60

checked hat
striped coat
spotted boots

Page 66

Do you have a bed?
Does your mom bring you warm milk?
Do you eat cookies too?

Students' questions will vary.

Page 68

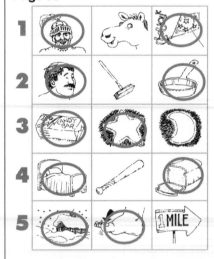

Page 72

to the football game
to the movies
to the zoo
answers will vary on last 2 items

Page 73

At a Football Game - football, goal posts
At the Movies - "Coming soon poster," theater seats
At the Zoo - sign to lions, cage

Page 78

Pictures in suitcase:
dinosaur pj top
toothbrush
blanket
teddy bear
socks
book
pillow

Page 80

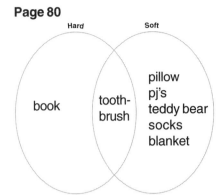

Hard   Soft

book   tooth-brush   pillow pj's teddy bear socks blanket

Page 84

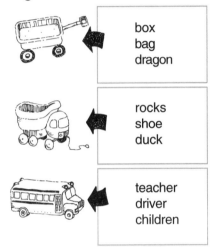

box
bag
dragon

rocks
shoe
duck

teacher
driver
children

Page 85
bag flag
tag drag
rag zag

a bean bag
a flag pole
a dish rag
a zigzag

Page 86
bag box
bus boot
dog man
cat cup
rug jar
tub ship

Page 90
1. Put in the mix.   2. Add the milk.
3. Put on the lid.   4. Shake it up.
5. Take off the lid.   6. Eat it up.

Page 92
Pictures on string:
swing
spring
ring
king
wing

Page 93
picture shows a cupcake with a candle

Page 96
pictures should show:
farm trucks - hay, animals, corn
big rigs - gas, food, cars
toy trucks - blocks, dolls, children

Page 97
pictures should show:
heavy - truck, rocks, books, wood
light - leaf, feathers, basket, flowers

Page 98

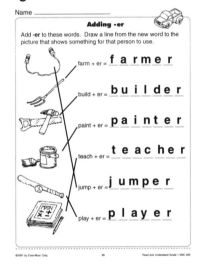

Page 102
in a forest or wooded area
camping, lying in a sleeping bag
the campfire is warm and the light
    makes the boy feel safe

Page 103
in the sleeping bag
on the fire
in the tent
in the forest

Page 108
Polar bear facts:
lives near North Pole
fur on bottom of feet
    keeps feet warm
    keeps from slipping
is a good swimmer
    paddles with front legs

Page 109
bear tear
wear pear

sentences:
bear
tear
wear
pear

Page 110
swimming
running
tapping
stopping
hitting
flipping
All the words have a double consonant and ing.

Page 111

Page 114
Sam lost his hat.
The hat ripped.

Page 115
First - mouse
Second - bunny
Third - fox
Fourth - goat
Fifth - ladybug

Page 116
bunny
goat
mouse
ladybug
ladybug
bunny
Sam

Page 120
to catch food
to stay safe

Animals   **Hiding Places**

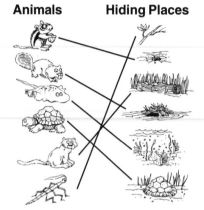

Page 121

Page 122

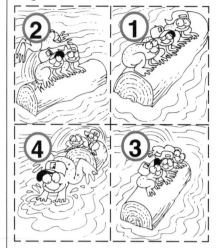

Page 126
lettuce, radishes, beets
pulled weeds, raked the soil
A garden is slow. Reasons will vary.

Page 127
placement of slant/plant and chant/
grant may be reversed

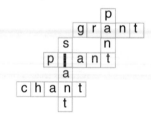

It was hot so the dog began to <u>pant</u>.
I wonder what seeds I should <u>plant</u>.
The girls jumped rope as they
shouted the <u>chant</u>.
The tower of blocks started to <u>slant</u>.

Page 128
1 - raking   2 - planting seeds
3 - watering   4 - picking lettuce

Page 129

dig up the potatoes

make ditches for watering

cut off the greens

smooth the soil

water the seeds

eat the salad

Page 132
It was a rainy (stormy) day.
Rhia was working at her computer.
Tania was working at her computer
    too; sending Rhia e-mail.
Rhia felt happy.
Tania will (smile, be happy, feel
    better)
Answers to last 2 items will vary.

Page 133

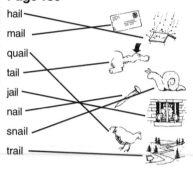

hail
mail
quail
tail
jail
nail
snail
trail

Page 134

Page 138
Ingredients:
bread   pickle
ham   lettuce

What to do:
1. Get a slice of bread.
2. Put a pickle on the slice of bread.
3. Put ham on top of the pickle.
4. Put lettuce on top of the ham.
5. Put another slice of bread on top.